THE MONTGOMERY BUS BOYCOTT

For two years after the United States Supreme Court ruled that public schools must be integrated with "all deliberate speed" there was little sign of any change in the segregated pattern of life in Montgomery, Alabama — the city that calls itself the Cradle of the Confederacy. But on the evening of December 1, 1955, a black seamstress refused to give up her bus seat to a white man. Arrested, tried, convicted, and fined about fourteen dollars, Mrs. Rosa Parks chose to appeal and to challenge the constitutionality of the Jim Crow law she had broken. United by a new leader, Dr. Martin Luther King, Jr., and a new philosophy, that of "nonviolent resistance," the Negro community organized the most successful bus boycott in history and opened a decade of struggle for first-class citizenship for blacks in all aspects of American life.

PRINCIPALS

Mrs. Rosa Parks, a middle-aged workingwoman of Montgomery, Alabama, who refused to give up her seat to a white man.

E. D. Nixon, trade unionist and NAACP leader who proposed the bus boycott in support of Mrs. Parks.

Fred Gray, a young black lawyer who represented Mrs. Parks and the Montgomery Improvement Association in the legal battles that went all the way to the United States Supreme Court.

Dr. Martin Luther King, Jr., pastor of the Dexter Avenue Baptist Church and president of the MIA — the leader and spokesman of the "movement."

Rev. Ralph Abernathy, another Baptist minister, a founder of the MIA and Dr. King's chief lieutenant.

The City Commissioners of Montgomery, the Police Commissioner, and the Mayor, representing the moderate but stubborn white segregationist majority.

Jack Crenshaw, attorney for the Montgomery City Lines, whose advice blocked a compromise solution.

John Blue Hill, a member of Alabama's most prominent political family, who acted as defense counsel for —

The Bombers, seven white men who confessed to wrecking four churches and two pastors' homes.

WHITE FRIENDS OF THE MIA, like Clifford and Virginia Durr, Rev. and Mrs. Robert Graetz, Joe Azbell, and many others, who felt as they did but could express their sympathy only anonymously.

THOUSANDS OF FRIENDS, BLACK AND WHITE, inside and outside the South, whose contributions of money and other support kept the movement from being starved out.

JUDGE RICHARD RIVES, presiding justice of the U.S. Circuit Court, Fifth District, who wrote the opinion which declared segregated seating unconstitutional.

THE WALKERS — thousands of humble, hardworking black people, many past middle age, who "walked with their heads up and their shoulders back, like they were seeing a new day," because they were the ones that brought it.

THE MONTGOMERY BUS BOYCOTT

Triumph in Montgomery, 1956. After 382 days of the boycott, black citizens of Montgomery were boarding newly integrated buses. (Wide World Photos)

A FOCUS BOOK

The Montgomery Bus Boycott, December, 1955

American Blacks Demand an End to Segregation

by Janet Stevenson

illustrated with photographs

FRANKLIN WATTS, INC.
845 Third Avenue, New York, N.Y. 10022

The authors and publisher of the Focus Books wish to acknowledge the helpful editorial suggestions of Professor Richard B. Morris.

SBN 531-00994-7
Copyright © 1971 by Franklin Watts, Inc.
Library of Congress Catalog Card Number: 73-161072
Printed in the United States of America
2 3 4 5 6

Contents

The Arrest of Rosa Parks	1
The Black Community Unites	11
Miracle on Monday Morning	19
"Hooked to the Stars..."	24
The Car Pools	27
The Opposition Toughens	32
The First Violence	35
The Boycott "Conspiracy"	38
To Raise the Federal Question	42
The Darkest Hour	47
"Be Ready When the Great Day Comes"	50
Backlash	55
The Final Act	58
Aftermath	59
Index	62

Mrs. Rosa Parks of Montgomery, Alabama, is shown here seated in the front of a city bus about a year after the boycott began. (United Press International)

The Arrest of Rosa Parks

On the evening of Thursday, December 1, 1955, a sweet-faced, neatly dressed black woman was riding home on a bus in Montgomery, Alabama. Mrs. Rosa Parks had put in a day's work at one of the downtown department stores. Her lap was full of groceries, which she would have to carry home from the bus stop, and already her feet and legs were tired.

Mrs. Parks was sitting in the row of seats directly behind the section marked "Whites Only." On runs where few, if any, white passengers got on, blacks could sit anywhere — except in the first ten seats. But if these were filled and more whites boarded the bus, drivers would order blacks to get up and give them their seats.

Some bus drivers went further in what seemed a deliberate attempt to make the daily bus ride as unpleasant and humiliating an experience as possible for those who made up almost three-quarters of the passengers on the Montgomery City Lines. Some drivers called blacks by ugly and insulting names. Some used any excuse to pick a quarrel and put the "offending" black passenger off.

One trick that was a favorite with certain drivers was particularly cruel. The company rule said that fares must be deposited in the coin box beside the driver, but that black passengers must board the bus from the rear. Blacks had to get on in front, drop their dimes in the box, then get off and go around to the back. The trick was to wait until the black passenger was between the two doors, then slam the doors shut and drive off, leaving him standing on the curb — minus his dime.

It had been played on Mrs. Parks more than once. Also, she knew all about the mistreatment other black people endured, for she had served as secretary of the Montgomery branch of the National Association for the Advancement of Colored People (NAACP). The most outspoken leader of that organization, E. D. Nixon, had been working for years to persuade the black community to unite in some sort of protest against conditions on the city bus lines. So far, his efforts had met with little success. But there were signs that a change was in the making.

Three times during this year of 1955, individual Negroes had refused to get up and give their seats to whites. All three were women. All had been arrested, jailed, and fined. Although there had been no broad support for any of the three, one of them — a high school student named Claudette Colvin — had won so much sympathy that a committee of black leaders had gone to discuss possible reforms with the city authorities and the manager of the bus lines.

The committee had requested more courtesy from the bus drivers and a statement of policy on seating from the bus company. The officials agreed to reprimand the bus drivers and to have the city attorney prepare a statement of seating policy.

But even this modest action was not taken. The bus company's lawyer, Jack Crenshaw, argued that the bus company needed the goodwill of the City Commission, which was soon to pass on renewal of its thirty-year franchise. Any action that disturbed the pattern of "Jim Crow" life in the city might cost it that goodwill. Besides, the law was clear, and the company must abide by it.*

No one knew all this recent history better than Mrs. Parks did, so she could hardly have hoped she was going to bring about any change in the state of affairs when she decided not to give up her seat to a white man who got on the bus halfway to her stop.

*Actually, the law was not clear. The city code had a provision that no passenger had to give up his seat if no other was available. The state law, which was not applicable inside Montgomery city limits, was the one Crenshaw advised the company to obey.

Three other black passengers who were also ordered by the driver to move back did so. They had to stand, for there were no longer any empty seats in the rear. Mrs. Parks had stood in that tight-packed aisle many times. But on this night she could not bring herself to do it. She sat where she was and looked out the window.

The driver looked back over his shoulder and called, "Niggers, move back!"

Mrs. Parks didn't move.

The driver pulled on his brake, got up, and pushed his way to where she sat. He repeated his order. She continued to stare out the window. There could be no doubt that she heard and was deliberately choosing to defy him. The driver got off the bus and came back with a policeman. Mrs. Parks was arrested and taken to the city jail.

No one — neither the driver, nor Rosa Parks, nor the white man who got her seat, nor E. D. Nixon, whose house Mrs. Parks telephoned from the jail — could possibly have guessed that at that moment the city which called itself the Cradle of the Confederacy was giving birth to a movement that was to change the pattern that had become known as the Southern way of life.

This pattern was not as old as many people believed. When blacks had been held as slaves, there were laws that discriminated against free blacks. But after the Civil War and the abolition of slavery, these laws were declared null and void. Other laws were passed — federal as well as state laws — making all Americans citizens and equal before the law. Black men could vote and hold office and sit on juries, just as white men could. Blacks could ride on trains and streetcars, use public buildings and parks, sit in churches and theaters, wherever whites could sit.

Some whites objected, and for years there had been a bitter struggle to keep the races separated as a matter of "local custom." Violence and terror were used against blacks who resisted, but blacks did resist

A representation of "Jim Crow." This symbol originated with a minstrel man named "Daddy" Rice who, in 1832, introduced a blackface act based on the capers of a slave by that name. Lyrics for the act went, in part, like this: "Weel a-bout and turn-a-bout! And ... jump Jim Crow ..." (Library of Congress)

— sometimes successfully for a time. But gradually the proponents of "white supremacy" were able to gain control of the legislatures of southern states and to pass the system of laws known by the nickname of Jim Crow.*

Between the years 1900 and 1907, every state below the Mason and Dixon's Line† passed laws prohibiting blacks from sitting in the same seats as whites on trains, streetcars, and other forms of public transportation; from going to school or church or the motion pictures together; from swimming at the same beaches; from playing in the same parks; or even from taking books from the same library shelves.

The laws were not the same in all parts of the South, nor were they always enforced with the same strictness. But in the first half of the twentieth century, Jim Crow was a basic fact of life in an area covering between one-third and one-half of the United States.

By 1950, however, there was a ground swell of black resistance that promised new conflict and change. One of the first clear signs of that change was the U.S. Supreme Court's decision in a suit challenging the "equality" of segregated schools. In *Brown v. Board of Education of Topeka* the high court ruled that such education was unequal by the very fact of being segregated and ordered all school systems to integrate "with all deliberate speed."

That was in 1954. There was an outcry against the decision in many parts of the South, and much argument about the meaning of the word "deliberate." Just how fast or how slow was "deliberate speed"?

A year later, it seemed that it was very slow indeed. By the end of

---

*The term is derived from a dance popular in old-time minstrel shows; it has come to stand for any pattern of living in which blacks are segregated from other Americans.

†A line establishing the southern border of Pennsylvania. It came to stand in the American public's mind for the border between free and slave territory.

The New York Times.

LATE CITY EDITION

VOL. CIII...No. 35,178.   NEW YORK, TUESDAY, MAY 18, 1954.   FIVE CENTS

HIGH COURT BANS SCHOOL SEGREGATION; 9-TO-0 DECISION GRANTS TIME TO COMPLY

McCarthy Hearing Off a Week as Eisenhower Bars Report

SENATOR IS IRATE

President Orders Aides Not to Disclose Details of Top-Level Meeting

President's letter and excerpts from transcript, Pages 24, 25, 26.

By W. H. LAWRENCE
Special to The New York Times.

WASHINGTON, May 17 — A secrecy directive by President Eisenhower resulted today in an abrupt recess for at least a week of the Senate's Army-McCarthy hearings.

Democratic and Republican Senators, some publicly and some privately, predicted that the investigation might never resume in earnest. However, there were other Senators who insisted that the investigation would go on to completion.

The recess was voted after Herbert Brownell Jr., the Attorney General, disclosed formally that criminal prosecutions might be instituted against those involved in the "preparation and dissemination" of an altered, condensed but still confidential Federal Bureau of Investigation report. This was offered in evidence last week by Senator Joseph R. McCarthy, Republican of Wisconsin.

Republicans outvoted Democrats 4 to 3 on the Senate Permanent Subcommittee of Investigation to recess the hearings until 10 o'clock next Monday morning. They acted amid charges and denials that the way was being prepared for a "white-wash."

Constitutional Division Cited

Communist Arms Unloaded in Guatemala By Vessel From Polish Port, U. S. Learns

State Department Views News Gravely Because of Red Infiltration

Special to The New York Times.
WASHINGTON, May 17 — The State Department said today that it had reliable information that "an important shipment of arms" had been sent from Communist-controlled territory to Guatemala.

It said the arms, now being unloaded at Puerto Barrios, Guatemala, had been shipped from Stettin, a former German Baltic seaport, which has been occupied by Communist Poland since World War II. The Guatemalan regime has been frequently accused of being influenced by Communists.

"Because of the point of origin of these arms, the point of their embarkation, their destination and the quantity of arms involved, the Department of State considers that this is a development of gravity," the announcement said. A freighter arrived at Puerto

Site of arms arrival (cross)

Barrios last Saturday, the State Department reported, carrying a large shipment of armament consigned to the Guatemalan Government.

The State Department did not divulge the exact quantity of the arms, their nature or where they had been manufactured.

Reliable sources told The New York Times, however, that ten freight car loads of goods listed in the manifest as "hardware" had been unloaded from this ship and sent to the City of Guatemala since Sunday. Guatemala is 150 miles from Puerto Barrios.

Continued on Page 10, Column 5

REACTION OF SOUTH

'Breathing Spell' for Adjustment Tempers Region's Feelings

By JOHN N. POPHAM
Special to The New York Times.
CHATTANOOGA, Tenn., May 17 — The South's reaction to the Supreme Court's decision outlawing racial segregation in public schools appeared to be tempered considerably today.

The time lag allowed for carrying out the required transitions seemed to be the major factor in that reaction.

Southern leaders of both races in political, educational and community service fields expressed comment that covered a wide range. Some spoke bitter words that verged on defiance. Others ranged from sharp disagreement to predictions of peaceful and successful adjustment in accord with the ruling.

But underneath the surface of much of the comment, it was evident that many Southerners recognized that the decision had laid down the legal principle rejecting segregation in public education facilities.

They also no'ed that it had left open a challenge to the region to join in working out a program of necessary changes in the present bi-racial school systems.

Three of the most illustrative viewpoints were those expressed by Govs. James F. Byrnes of South Carolina and Herman Talmadge of Georgia, and Harold Fleming, a spokesman for the Southern Regional Council, an interracial organi-

LEADERS IN SEGREGATION FIGHT: Lawyers who led battle before U. S. Supreme Court for abolition of segregation in public schools congratulate one another as they leave court after announcement of decision. Left to right: George E. C. Hayes, Thurgood Marshall and James M. Nabrit.

1896 RULING UPSET

'Separate but Equal' Doctrine Held Out of Place in Education

Text of Supreme Court decision is printed on Page 15.

By LUTHER A. HUSTON
Special to The New York Times.
WASHINGTON, May 17 — The Supreme Court unanimously outlawed today racial segregation in public schools.

Chief Justice Earl Warren read two opinions that put the stamp of unconstitutionality on school systems in twenty-one states and the District of Columbia where segregation is permissive or mandatory.

The court, taking cognizance of the problems involved in the integration of the school systems concerned, put over until the next term, beginning in October, the formulation of decrees to effectuate its 9-to-0 decision.

The opinions set aside the "separate but equal" doctrine laid down by the Supreme Court in 1896.

"In the field of public education," Chief Justice Warren said, "the doctrine of 'separate but equal' has no place. Separate educational facilities are inherently unequal."

He stated the question and supplied the answer as follows:

"We come then to the question presented: Does segregation of children in public schools solely on the basis of race, even though physical facilities and other 'tangible' factors may be equ-

SOVIET BIDS VIENNA CEASE 'INTRIGUES'

Envoy Warns Austrian Chief on Inciting East Zone — Raab Denies Charges

By JOHN MacCORMAC
Special to The New York Times.
VIENNA, May 17 — The Soviet Union warned Austria today to put an end to "hostile and subversive intrigues" against the Soviet occupation forces, or Soviet authorities would do it themselves.

Ivan I.

City Colleges' Board Can't Pick Chairman

The Board of Higher Education was unable to elect a chairman at its annual meeting last night at Hunter College.

A spokesman said it was the first time "within memory of board officials" that such a situation had occurred.

Nineteen of the twenty-one members of the board, which governs the four municipal colleges, attended.

Two members nominated for the one-year-term were unable to attain the required majority of eleven votes. T.ey were Joseph B. Cavallaro, who was up for re-election as chairman, and Dr. Harry J. Carman, who was restored to the

2 TAX PROJECTS DIE IN ESTIMATE BOARD

Beer Levy and More Parking Collections Killed — Payroll Impost Still Weighed

By CHARLES G. BENNETT
Two possible new revenue sources were definitely eliminated yesterday by the Board of Estimate in executive session. They were the proposed 1-cent-a-glass tax on beer and the suggestion to extend metered parking

MORETTIS' LAWYER MUST BARE TALKS

Jersey Court Orders Counsel in Racket

RULING TO FIGURE IN '54 CAMPAIGN

Decision Tied to Eisenhower "Leads Southerners"

New York Times *headlines announce the famous decision by the Supreme Court in the* Brown v. Board of Education *case.* (Courtesy, New York Times)

1955, although petitions asking desegregation had been filed by Negro parents in 170 southern school districts, not even token integration had begun anywhere except in the District of Columbia and in a few border states. Other forms of segregation had hardly even been tested.

Members of NAACP branches in many southern cities had been discussing ways and means of making such tests. Lawsuits were one way, but they were expensive and slow. Economic pressure was another way. Since many stores and transportation systems depended heavily on Negroes' patronage, they were logical targets for that kind of pressure. If blacks didn't ride buses and didn't buy in stores where they were badly treated, things might change. And change for the better!

This was not an original idea. Back in the early 1900's, black people all over the South had refused to ride on streetcars with "Whites Only" sections. In a number of places they had forced streetcar companies and city authorities to back down. But only for a time. Eventually Jim Crow had triumphed, and few southerners, black or white, even knew of the old boycott movements.

The man who first proposed the Montgomery boycott of 1955 had never heard of the successful Montgomery boycott of 1900–1902.*

E. D. Nixon, son of a sharecropper in Autauga County, came to Montgomery as a young man and got a job as a Pullman car porter. Traveling to other parts of the country, he saw other "ways of life." Through his trade union, he gained experience of a kind he would never have had on a poverty-stricken farm in rural Alabama. Nixon put this experience to work on the critical problems that faced his fellow black citizens.

He helped organize and served as president of the Alabama State

---

*cf. Meier and Rudwick, *The Black Experience in America*, University of Texas Press, Austin, 1970, p. 91.

E. D. Nixon, NAACP leader who proposed the bus boycott in support of Mrs. Parks. (EBONY Magazine)

and Montgomery branches of the NAACP. Much of the NAACP's work in this period was the defense of individual blacks who were unable to get "equal and exact justice" in southern courts. But Nixon believed the organization ought to work in wider fields as well.

In the Brotherhood of Sleeping Car Porters, he had often heard the word "solidarity." Union leaders spoke of winning over seemingly impossible odds as long as men who needed the same things stood solidly together. Black Montgomery needed relief from the twice daily ordeal of riding on Jim Crow buses. Nixon was convinced that if 50,000 black Montgomerians would stand solidly together for even a single day, the bus company would learn an important lesson. At the very least, there would be some effort to discipline hostile and discourteous drivers.

But that sort of solidarity seemed almost impossible to achieve. There were too many differences within the black community: differences of religious faith, education, standard of living, and political opinion, as well as personality. The upper class was a comparatively large one, made up of professors,* teachers, doctors, dentists, and successful businessmen, many of whom felt that they had little in common with domestic workers and laborers. They went to different churches, belonged to different clubs, recognized different leaders. Some of these leaders were considered "Uncle Toms" by such militants as E. D. Nixon. But without the help of the educated, economically secure "elite," very little could be accomplished by Montgomery's poor and uneducated blacks.

Since March, 1955, when the community's first effort to protest (around the case of Claudette Colvin) had met with frustration, there had been more ferment than usual in all sections of the black community, and more contact between them. There had been more activity, also, in the Council on Human Relations, where a few courageous whites and a few of the black professionals got together, simply to keep some channel of communications open between the races. In all these quarters, it was agreed that some action would have to be taken soon, that it must involve the entire black community, and that it must be headed by strong and able leaders.

But what action? Under what leaders? And on what case?

Mrs. Rosa Parks's act of defiance was a partial answer to those questions.

In fact, many critics of the "movement" said from the start that it was no accident that Mrs. Parks had been arrested. She had been

---

*Alabama State College, a large, predominantly black institution, is located in Montgomery.

"planted," they said, just because she was an ideal person around whom to organize community support. She had spent many hours of many days riding around the city "trying to get herself arrested" for not moving back.

The only truth in this rumor was that Mrs. Parks was an ideal personality for a test of the law. She was hardworking, highly respected, active in her church and in other groups in the black community. Married, but childless, she lived with and supported her invalid mother by sewing, a skill which she had learned at Miss White's school for Negro girls in South Montgomery. (Miss White's was one of the many "academies" founded after the Civil War by New England "schoolmarms" to educate the newly freed black youth. Graduates of Miss White's had the reputation of being not only well educated and well trained in domestic arts, but also young women with a high sense of personal dignity.)

Gentle, unassuming, but profoundly courageous, Mrs. Parks inspired by example. If this frail, middle-aged woman could stand her ground against injustice and bullying, who could respect himself if he did less?

When she was taken off to jail, one of the three important questions was thus answered. But there were still two others. What action should the community take in support of Mrs. Parks? And who was going to lead that action?

The Black Community Unites

When E. D. Nixon got home that evening, his wife told him that Mrs. Parks was being held in the city jail.

Nixon called and asked on what charge, and at what bail, but the desk sergeant refused to tell him. (Nixon was considered a troublemaker by some local law enforcement officials, and there was no legal reason why anyone not officially connected with a prisoner should be given such information.)

As a next step, Nixon would ordinarily have called one of the two black attorneys then practicing in Montgomery, a young man named Fred Gray, who had already showed both ability and courage in the defense of blacks who had got in some sort of trouble with the law. But Gray was out of town and was not expected back until late Sunday or early Monday.

In this emergency, Nixon turned to a white attorney, Clifford Durr, member of a family that had lived in Montgomery County for nearly two hundred years. Both Clifford Durr and his wife were members of the Council on Human Relations and had been helpful to Nixon and Gray in legal matters. Also, Mrs. Parks sometimes helped Mrs. Durr with the sewing for the Durrs' high-school-age daughters, and the two women had become friends.

Assuming, no doubt, that Durr was going to represent Mrs. Parks, the desk sergeant explained the charge and said bail had been set at fifty dollars. Half an hour later, the Durrs and Nixon were at the jail arranging for Mrs. Parks's release. At Nixon's request, Durr had the hearing set in the recorder's court for the following Monday. (Nixon had to be out of town on his "run" from Friday afternoon until sometime Sunday. Also Gray would not be back until then.)

Over coffee at Mrs. Parks's home, the little group listened to her account of what had occurred. "I had no intention of doing any such thing when I got on the bus," she said. "I was just bone weary. And I knew I was going to be more weary when I'd walked home, carrying those bags. So when that driver told me to get up and let that man sit down, I just wasn't going to do it."

Durr asked a few questions and then gave Mrs. Parks this advice. "I think I can get you off on the 'facts' if you want me to represent you and want to go about things in that way," he said, and explained the special proviso in the city code that no one had to give up a seat if no other was available. "But that will not test the segregation law.

"If that's what you want to do, you must be prepared for a long, expensive fight. You'll lose in the local court, and you'll lose on appeal. But you must go through the appeals procedure before you can get to the U.S. Supreme Court and 'raise the federal question.'

"When you've done all that, of course, there's no guarantee that the U.S. Supreme Court will hear your case, but there's a chance. Maybe a good chance.

"If you want to make the try, you'll need all the help you can get from some big, national organization like the NAACP. In that case, you ought to ask Fred Gray to represent you. Think about it. Talk to him when he gets back. And let me know what you decide."

When E. D. Nixon got home that night, Mrs. Nixon was waiting to hear how it had all turned out.

"I think we've got our test case," her husband said. "What we've got to think about now is getting folks to stay off the buses so we can go at this thing from both ends."

"You know people aren't going to stay off the buses in the middle of winter," said his wife.

"We'll see. Maybe winter's the best time to begin. If we can get them to stay off while it's cold, there won't be any trouble about keeping them off later on."

Mrs. Nixon smiled and shook her head. "If headaches were selling for a dollar a dozen, you're the guy who'd walk into the drugstore and ask them to give you a dollar's worth."

Early next morning, Nixon was on the telephone. He had drawn up a list of prominent citizens from which he hoped to form the nucleus of a new organization. He himself could not attend the first gathering of the group, but he had taken the initiative of setting the time and place. It was to be late in the afternoon, when most people had finished their day's work, at the Dexter Avenue Baptist Church. This was centrally located, and it was the church of Montgomery's black professional class. Also, its new pastor, Dr. Martin Luther King, Jr., of Atlanta, was a leader on whom Nixon had had his eye for several months.

The first name on Nixon's telephone list was Rev. Ralph Abernathy, of the First Baptist Church, a vigorous young minister with whom Nixon had worked on other campaigns. Abernathy agreed that a meeting should be called to plan community action, and that a leaflet should be prepared at once, announcing a one-day boycott of the buses and a mass meeting to follow on Monday evening.

With Abernathy's encouragement, Nixon next called Rev. H. H. Hubbard, head of the Baptist Ministerial Alliance. This is the largest denomination in the black community and cooperation by its leadership was absolutely essential. Hubbard was as enthusiastic as Abernathy and authorized the notification of all Baptist ministers in the city. Nixon next called young Dr. King. He, too, was sympathetic and agreed to the use of his church for the informal planning meeting, but he asked for a little time to think over his own participation. Nixon promised to call him back and went on down his list.

The Dexter Avenue Baptist Church in Montgomery, Alabama. (Wide World Photos)

There was Rev. L. Roy Bennett, head of the Interdenominational Ministerial Alliance, which included all the other Protestant groups. Bennett agreed to call some of his colleagues and to chair the Friday meeting. There was Mrs. Jo Ann Robinson, of the Alabama State College faculty and the Women's Political Council. She agreed to write the leaflet and to get it mimeographed and distributed by the women of her group. And so on and on. The response to every call was positive.

By the time Nixon called Dr. King again, the latter had decided that he did want to take an active part in the effort. He had been concerned, he admitted now, about the justice as well as the wisdom of a boycott, and he had been uncertain that his own schedule gave him time for still another "outside activity." He did not know Mrs. Parks personally. But what he knew of her convinced him that hers was the case with the best chance of uniting the community, and he believed that a boycott was the best way to support it.

More than forty people gathered in the big meeting room at the Dexter Avenue Baptist Church Friday afternoon. Most of them were ministers, but there were men and women representing many other walks of life.

There was immediate agreement on the one-day boycott. But what about the next day? And the next? How would people get to and from work if the protest was continued? Some felt the best thing to do was to call it off after "showing our strength" and leave it to the negotiating committee to force concessions on the threat of a repetition. Others felt that no amount of negotiation would bring about any important change, that only a severe economic pinch would teach the company where its interests lay.

The final decision, of course, would have to be made by the people who would carry it out: the workingmen and workingwomen of the black community. They would have a chance to express their feelings at the mass meeting, which was now scheduled for Monday at 7:00 P.M., in the largest black church in the city.

The informal gathering now concentrated on the urgent problem of how to get word spread throughout the community. There was no guarantee that the thousands of blacks who lived many miles from their jobs were going to stay off the bus Monday morning, just because a group of self-appointed leaders said they ought to. But unless they knew of the boycott movement, there was no chance they would cooperate.

Unfortunately, there was no Negro "ghetto" in Montgomery. Blacks lived in all parts of the city and its surrounding countryside. A telephone campaign could not reach everyone. Many had no phones and took no newspapers. Leaflets passed out at the stores where families did their week's shopping on Saturday would reach many thousands. Announcements made from church pulpits on Sunday would reach even more.

All the ministers present were willing to make such announcements and to urge their congregations to join the protest. The Reverend Mr. Bennett promised to notify key members of the Interdenominational Ministerial Alliance and to ask them to pass the word along.

So other, smaller meetings were arranged for, meetings at which one or two of those present at this first gathering would undertake to rally support from a larger circle. And a committee was formed to draw up a shorter version of Mrs. Robinson's leaflet. Dr. King had volunteered the use of his church mimeograph machine to make seven thousand copies of this flyer for city-wide distribution. It read as follows:

Don't ride the bus to work, to town, to school, or any place Monday, December 5.

Another Negro woman has been arrested and put in jail because she refused to give up her bus seat.

Don't ride the buses to work, to town, to school, or anywhere on Monday. If you work, take a cab, or share a ride, or walk.

Come to a mass meeting, Monday, at 7:00 P.M., at the Holt Street Baptist Church for further instruction.

The most serious obstacle to the success of the Monday action was touched on in those phrases, "take a cab, or share a ride, or walk." It was not going to be easy for hundreds and hundreds of people to do that. Someone suggested that the Negro-owned taxicab companies might be willing to make a special arrangement: drivers might pick up pedestrians on the street that morning and carry them to their jobs for the dime they would have paid on the bus. A committee was formed to get in touch with the companies.*

Under the circumstances, it looked as if even 50 percent effectiveness would be hard to achieve. But cutting the company's revenues in half would be an impressive lesson in economics. Anything better than that would be a real victory and cause for rejoicing. With luck, 60 percent or even 65 percent effectiveness was possible.

And luck was already working on the side of the protest.

As E. D. Nixon went to the station to board his Pullman car that afternoon, he met a reporter from the *Montgomery Advertiser*. Joe Azbell had frequently expressed sympathy with the grievances of the black community, and on an impulse Nixon offered him a "scoop." If Azbell would promise to write an accurate story without degrading or insulting overtones, Nixon would let him in on a sensational secret.

Azbell promised.

Nixon told him what had happened to Mrs. Parks and what was

---

*There were 18 Negro-owned companies in Montgomery, and 210 Negro drivers. Segregation was so complete at that time that these cabs had to be marked "Colored" and could not pick up white passengers.

planned in the way of a protest. So that the reporter could print the details of the proposed boycott without revealing his source, Nixon suggested that he get hold of one of the leaflets and make up whatever explanation he liked about how it came into his possession.*

Sunday morning's *Advertiser* carried a front-page, two-column story with the full text of the leaflet. It was complete and accurate as Azbell had promised. The tone of shocked indignation made it "fit to print" by the publisher's standards, but did not frighten off the paper's black readership. If there was a minister in Montgomery who had not heard the news or who was not yet convinced that the action was going to be widely supported, he knew better now.

Many carried the newspaper into the pulpit with them to be sure that their announcement was correct in all details.

Also on Sunday morning, the city's police commissioner went on the radio with an announcement that two motorcycle policemen would follow every bus on Monday morning's schedule to protect those who wished to ride from possible harassment by "goon squads." Montgomery Negroes were not accustomed to the police in the role of protectors, and the announcement may well have kept many away from the bus stops.

*Nixon and Azbell respected each other's confidence, and the true story of Azbell's "scoop" was not known even among leaders of the movement for many years. One story that circulated was that Azbell had picked up a leaflet from the sidewalk. Another was that a Negro maid who couldn't read had taken her copy to her white employer, who had given it to the *Advertiser* to warn the white community of "what the Negroes were up to."

Miracle on Monday Morning

Monday, December 5, was a dull, chilly day. The sky was still dark when the first buses began to roll.

By 6:00 A.M. early risers could look out their windows and see the lighted buses go by. They were empty, or almost empty, of Negro passengers!

There were a few whites — the usual number — and here and there a single black, someone who had been away over the weekend and had missed the news. Behind each bus there rode the motorcycle escort promised by Police Commissioner Sellers. But there were no "goon squads" in sight.

As the sky brightened, the sidewalks were crowded with an unusual number of black pedestrians. College and high school students were thumbing rides. Now and then a man riding a mule caused a ripple of laughter among the walkers. There were even a few old-fashioned, horse-drawn buggies, which looked as if they might have been left over from the shooting of the film *Gone with the Wind*.

Dr. King and other leaders got in their cars and cruised the Negro neighborhoods all over the city. Everywhere it was the same. The buses were running empty. People were walking and seeming to enjoy it. They waved to the leaders they recognized. Students cheered the empty buses. Quite a number were singing as they walked.

At 9:30 A.M. Mrs. Parks appeared in the courtroom with her attorney, Fred Gray.

The charge against her was still violation of the *city*'s segregation statute, and Gray could have taken the line suggested by Clifford Durr and defended her on the grounds that no other seat was available. But Mrs. Parks had decided to do all she could to test the constitutionality of the basic idea of segregation. In one sense, she was lucky that the charge against her was honestly based on that law and was not the usual "disorderly conduct" or "disturbing the peace" charge so often used in this type of arrest.

Gray's defense attacked the city and state laws requiring segregated seating, on the grounds that they violated the letter and spirit of the federal constitution. The judge found Mrs. Parks guilty and fined her ten dollars and court costs, which amounted to four dollars. Gray said his client would appeal the verdict, and Mrs. Parks was again released on bond.

By the middle of the day, the boycott had succeeded beyond anyone's most optimistic hopes. Morale was high in the black community, and it looked as if the mass meeting was going to be very well attended. A planning meeting had been called for 3:00 P.M. to settle the details of the program and to prepare a set of recommendations for a vote by the audience.

"We're going to need a permanent organization," E. D. Nixon said to two of his friends as they left the courtroom after Mrs. Parks's hearing. "We ought to decide on a name, a slate of officers, and a set of demands."

"Can't we do that at this afternoon's meeting?" asked Ralph Abernathy.

"We can. But we'll get more done if we go there with some suggestions," said Nixon.

So he and Abernathy and the third man, Rev. E. N. French, constituted themselves an "agenda committee" and began to work out a preliminary set of proposals. First, there was the matter of a name. Nixon suggested something like a "Citizens' Council," but Abernathy objected. It sounded too much like the White Citizens' Councils, which had been organizing in opposition to the Supreme Court's school integration order. After some discussion, the three agreed on Abernathy's suggestion of the "Montgomery Improvement Association."

Next came the question of leadership.

"We all expect you to serve as president, Brother Nixon," said Abernathy. "Are you willing?"

"Not unless you turn down the man I want to propose."

"Who is that?"

"Martin Luther King, Jr."

Both the ministers were surprised. Dr. King was new to Montgomery, and there were a number of other ministers, as well as laymen active in political affairs, who were more obvious choices for the top post. But Nixon had some impressive arguments for his choice.

There was, for instance, the young man's outstanding talent as an orator. "First time I heard him preach," Nixon said, "I turned to the fellow sitting next to me and I said, 'I don't know how I'm going to do it, but some day I'm going to hook him to the stars!'"

Also, Dr. King would be able to talk to the white power structure in their own language. He had been educated at Morehouse College in Atlanta, at Crozer Theological Seminary, and at Boston University, where he had been granted a doctor's degree. Finally, he had not been in Montgomery long enough to become entangled in any of the factional fights that divided the black community.

In his own case, Nixon acknowledged that he had made many enemies, that he was hampered by a poor education, and that he had to be out of the city more than he was in it because of the nature of his work. "And we're going to need a full-time president!"

"I'll go along with your nomination," said Abernathy, "but are you sure Dr. King will?"

Nixon was not sure, but he thought the best way to persuade him was to present his name at the afternoon planning meeting and ask him

Dr. Martin Luther King, Jr., speaking at the Holt Street Baptist Church in Montgomery during the boycott. (Wide World Photos)

to accept or refuse on the spot. Other nominations were jotted down on a slip of paper. French agreed to accept the post of corresponding secretary, and Nixon, that of treasurer. Abernathy would serve as head of whatever committee was formed to carry on the negotiation with the authorities. From those present at the afternoon meeting an executive board could be selected large enough to represent all sections of the community — with a special place of honor for Mrs. Rosa Parks.

The afternoon meeting accepted these suggestions. Martin Luther King was taken by surprise and unanimously elected before he had time to think through his feeling about such a responsibility.* A set of three demands was agreed upon: a guarantee of courtesy from the bus drivers; a "first-come, first-served" seating policy; and jobs for black drivers on predominantly black runs. And the discussion moved on to the critical question: What course of action should be recommended to the audience at the mass meeting — to continue the boycott, or to "quit while we're ahead"?

There was the same division of opinion as before. It was pointed out that the morning's magnificent showing might not be repeated at the end of the day. Any sign of weakness would convince the power structure that it had only to hold out and the boycott would fizzle out. It would be better to call it off than to let it evaporate. The negotiating committee could always use the threat of another riders' "strike" to pressure the authorities if they had not been sufficiently impressed.

Probably a majority of those present now believed that it was better to keep the momentum of the morning's 99 percent miracle, and to urge the audience at the mass meeting to keep up what they had begun so well. But the exact phrasing of the recommendation was left to Dr. King, whose role as president of the Montgomery Improvement Association included the delivery of the evening's main address.

*Dr. King wrote in *Stride Toward Freedom* that if he had had more time he would probably have declined, as he had just declined the presidency of the Montgomery branch of the NAACP to give himself time to learn the duties of his first full-time pastorate.

"Hooked to the Stars..."

By the time the afternoon meeting was over, every seat in the Holt Street Baptist Church was filled by people who had come early to be sure of getting in.

The host minister, Rev. A. W. Wilson, had arranged for a loudspeaker system to be set up on the roof, so that latecomers who could not find seats would be able to hear all that went on. By 6:30 P.M. it seemed even that would not be enough. Several thousand men and women were standing in front of, and on all sides of the church, in the street on which it faced, and in all side streets within three or four blocks.

By 6:45 speakers could hardly get through to the entrance door. Dr. King was half an hour late because of the crowd. Mrs. Parks, E. D. Nixon, and others who had been nominated for office were on the platform as the meeting finally got under way with the singing of an old hymn whose verses seemed to have taken on new meaning:

"Onward, Christian soldiers,
Marching as to war! . . ."

There were prayers, scripture readings, and a formal presentation of Mrs. Parks, who received a standing ovation from the packed house. E. D. Nixon spoke in his usual forceful manner.

"Before you brothers and sisters get comfortable in your seats, I want to say if anybody here is afraid, he better take his hat and go home. This is going to be a long-drawn-out affair, and before it's over, somebody's going to die!

"But we've worn aprons too long! It's time for us to take them off!"

Nixon was applauded as if there were no one present who understood the meaning of the word "fear." Police Commissioner Sellers was sitting in the audience, and Nixon could see him clearly. He was not applauding, but he was not missing the message of the applause he heard.

Dr. King was introduced and came forward. He was — for perhaps the first time in his career — almost totally unprepared; there had been no time in the two hours since he had learned that this duty was to be his. All he had been able to do was gather his thoughts enough to decide that his speech must make two mutually contradictory appeals.

For Dr. King understood the anger and bitterness in the hearts of those who would hear him, and he believed it was his duty to drain off those negative emotions. He also knew how high a courage would be needed for the ordeal ahead, and he believed it was his duty to fan the fire of such courage. He had to be militant and moderate at the same time. He doubted his own ability to perform that sort of oratorical feat.

As he gripped the rostrum to steady himself, television lights were turned on and cameras began to whir. The day's events had already focused national attention on Montgomery. The sense of history in the making gripped everyone present and even those in the streets outside.

Dr. King began by telling what had happened to Mrs. Parks, putting it into the context of the long, long history of such incidents, not only in Montgomery, but all over the South.

"But there comes a time when people get tired," he said. "And we are here this evening to say to those who have mistreated us so long that we are tired — tired of being segregated and humiliated, tired of being kicked about by the brutal feet of oppression.

"For many years, we have shown amazing patience. We have sometimes given our white brothers the feeling that we liked the way we were being treated. But we came here tonight to be saved from that patience that makes us patient with anything less than freedom and justice."

Here he was interrupted with applause so loud that he had to wait for it to quiet down before he could go on. Next, he outlined in clear, careful words the kind of protest that was being proposed. "There will be no threats or intimidation. We will only say to people, 'Let your conscience be your guide.' Once again we must hear the words of Jesus echoing across the centuries: 'Love your enemies, bless them that curse you, and pray for them that despitefully use you. . . .'

"In spite of the mistreatment that we have confronted, we must not become bitter and end up by hating our white brothers."

King paused to see whether his audience would accept this challenge as they had accepted his call to protest. The applause was every bit as loud. Reassured that he had somehow managed to strike the delicate balance he hoped for, Dr. King went on to his final plea.

"If you will protest courageously and yet with dignity and Christian love, when the history books are written in future generations, the historians will have to pause and say, 'There lived a great people — a black people — who injected new meaning and dignity into the veins of civilization.' This is our challenge and our overwhelming responsibility."

He had spoken "with the tongues of men and angels." Indeed, some of the deeply religious people who heard him claimed afterward to have seen angels standing around him, lifting him on their wings. As his words soared, so did the spirit of all who heard him. Thousands upon thousands of plain people accepted the burden he laid on them and would bear it for month after weary month.

Long before Abernathy put the question of the evening to a vote, the result was clear. They were going to stay off the buses until the demands voiced by their leaders were met.

The Car Pools

On Thursday, December 8, the MIA negotiating committee met with the City Commission and representatives of the Montgomery City Lines to discuss those demands. As before, the company's attorney expressed the opinion that the company must abide by the Alabama law. That would have to be changed before company policy could change.

The compromise plan was rejected, and the way paved for a much more basic reform.

One reason for the stubbornness of the authorities in the face of three days of almost total boycott — an unheard-of achievement in the history of such movements — was a card they believed they could play whenever they liked.

The boycott movement depended from the beginning on there being some other way of getting working people to their jobs. The bulk of Montgomery's bus riders were poor and supported large families. They couldn't afford to lose a single day's wage by failing to show up for work. Negro taxi drivers were providing the only real alternative to the bus system, and cabdrivers were subject to city control.

There was a law regulating taxi fares. Any driver operating on a city license had to obey that law. Drivers who were carrying passengers for a dime were "undercharging," and could be threatened with the loss of their operator's license.

Someone at the Thursday negotiating meeting dropped a hint that some such move was on the city's agenda. Dr. King caught the hint, and as soon as he got home, he put in a long-distance call to a friend in Baton Rouge, Louisiana. There had been a bus boycott in that city and, as he hoped, Dr. King's friend was able to give an account of the organization of a volunteer car pool, big enough to care for hundreds, if not thousands, of ex-bus-riders at a minimum cost.

At this point, the organizational ability that had been developing over many years in the segregated black community began to pay dividends. A transportation committee was formed under the leadership of a businessman named Rufus Lewis. Dr. King gave his notes on the Baton Rouge plan to Lewis, who went to work with his committee to adapt it to the local situation.

There was a regular mass meeting scheduled for each Monday and Thursday evening, to keep up morale, to get news around, to squelch rumors, and to permit the discussion and ratification of decisions. At the very first of these meetings, Thursday, December 8, there was a preliminary appeal for volunteer drivers, to be ready in case of a sudden crackdown on the taxicabs. At the end of the meeting, the transportation committee had a list of 150 people who had cars and were willing to drive people to and from work.

The emergency arose not quite twenty-four hours later, when a formal warning was issued to all cab companies, reminding them that the legal minimum fare was forty-five cents, and that failure to charge it was a punishable offense.

That was Friday, the end of the working week for many. On Saturday, volunteer drivers cruised the streets picking up anyone who flagged them down. On Sunday, ministers announced that more volunteers were needed. The list was doubled to three hundred that day.

Some of those who signed up could drive only a few hours before and after their own work. Others were willing to drive all day long, as for example, Mrs. A. W. West. This elderly widow of a successful dentist was the dowager of the black community, and her big green Cadillac was pressed into service from the start of the car pools. She drove from before dawn until after dark all through those first tense winter months and kept up her good work until her car was literally worn out.

With these forces at their command, the transportation committee tackled the planning of a system that would get 17,500 people back and forth to work every day. It was a job the bus company had never done to everyone's satisfaction. But Rufus Lewis was not discouraged. He took some cues from the Baton Rouge experience and some from his committee members' knowledge of Montgomery, and together they created a network of "dispatch" and "pickup" stations that covered the town.

The dispatch stations were located in those neighborhoods where large numbers of black people lived. They were to be open only in the mornings, from 6:00 until 10:00. The pickup stations were harder to locate. To be used by people returning from work, they had to be either in the downtown area or in white residential neighborhoods. Black churches opened their doors to shelter riders waiting at dispatch stations, but the pickup stations were in unfriendly territory, and open from 3:00 P.M. until 7:00 P.M., which was the time of the general rush hour.

The most important pickup station was finally located in a Negro-owned parking lot in the center of town. Here a special dispatcher was assigned to group passengers in such a way as to keep the cars as full and the runs as short as possible. Another vital center was a drugstore owned by a Negro pharmacist.

By Tuesday, December 13, just a week after the boycott began, the transportation committee had thousands of mimeographed leaflets ready for distribution, showing the location of forty-eight dispatch stations and forty-two pickup stations. Cars were to be assigned to these in numbers that would depend on how heavily each station was used in the first few days.

The system worked amazingly well, although it was not perfect. Individual drivers and passengers were sometimes hard to deal with.

During the boycott, this church-operated station wagon provided transportation for black citizens boycotting segregated city buses. (Wide World Photos)

Cars sometimes broke down. And even when everything was going smoothly, there was never enough space for everyone who had formerly ridden the buses. Many people began walking to work on December 5 and kept it up all through the winter and spring. For elderly women who worked as domestics in private homes this was a real hardship, but they did it with pride.

Help came from some unexpected sources in those first weeks. Many whites, who were sympathetic but timid about saying so in public, began to stop and offer lifts to black people they knew, and even to those they didn't know. Housewives who didn't want their maids to arrive too tired to work began to drive them back and forth. When the mayor appealed to them to stop giving "aid and comfort" to the boycott in this way, the ladies fell back on the myth of the "goon squads" that were supposed to be harassing defenseless women who wanted nothing to do with the boycott. Neither maids nor mistresses believed this myth, but it was a solid excuse for doing what they were doing.

Very substantial help came from outside Montgomery in the form of more than a dozen brand-new station wagons, donated by church and other groups to black churches that were participating in the movement. This was the result of national news coverage of the boycott, and of campaigns by the NAACP, religious denominations, and trade unions to spread the "message of Montgomery" and recruit support from one end of the country to the other.

Financial support was also important. Gasoline and oil cost money. So did telephones. There were supplies for leaflets to be bought, moving expenses (as the MIA was ousted from first one office and then another), travel expenses for leaders going out of state on speaking tours, insurance on cars and station wagons, legal fees, court costs, and so on. Collections were taken at every mass meeting, but the movement could never have supported itself on the contributions of the ex-riders themselves.

One of the most impressive achievements of the MIA was that it raised what it needed by voluntary contributions, most of them unsolicited, without ever making a public appeal for funds. Money came from as far away as Singapore in one direction and Switzerland in the other. Contributions were brought by visitors who came to see for themselves what was happening, some in single dollar bills, others in checks as large as five thousand dollars. All in all, the MIA collected nearly a quarter of a million dollars.

The Opposition Toughens

Important as money and moral support from outside were to the success of the movement, it was the unity of the black community that kept its heart pumping. Recognizing this fact, the city authorities directed their next attacks at that unity. A concerted effort had been made by white religious leaders to persuade Dr. King and the other ministers that it was their Christian duty to call off the boycott during the Christmas period as a gesture of goodwill. It was hinted that such a gesture would be rewarded more generously than stubborn insistence on "unreasonable demands." When this did not work, there was an attempt to divide and confuse the black community by setting up a rival leadership.

On Sunday, January 22, there was a story in the *Advertiser* to the effect that the City Commission had met with "three prominent Negro ministers," who had agreed to the terms of a settlement of the boycott. It was, therefore, to be cancelled as of the following (Monday) morning. This hoax might have worked — at least it might have worked well enough to break the 99-percent-effective record of which the black community was so justly proud — but news of the article was "leaked" to the MIA leaders before it appeared.

They went to work to identify the "three prominent ministers" (who turned out to be not prominent at all) and to get sworn denials from them that they had even discussed a settlement. All three said they had been invited to City Hall to discuss something connected with a new type of insurance for the city. Meanwhile, a group of volunteers made the rounds of Montgomery's nightclubs on Saturday, publicizing the falsehood of the story before it even appeared. Ministers denounced the lie from their pulpits on Sunday. And on Monday, the buses rolled along the streets as empty as ever.

The attack moved back to the car pools. It began with petty harassments of the volunteer drivers. They were pulled over and given tickets for speeding and other alleged violations. Sometimes they were arrested and taken to jail where they had to post bail before being released. Riders waiting to be picked up at dispatch stations were reminded of the laws against "hitchhiking" and vagrancy. As some of the volunteer drivers were frightened into dropping out, the busy MIA officers had to take turns on relief duty. Martin Luther King was one of those who drove whenever he had a spare half hour.

One morning he was stopped at a dispatch station and asked to show his license and owner's papers. His car was followed by two motorcycle policemen, and after a few blocks, one of them arrested him for going 30 miles an hour in a 25-mile zone. He was ordered out of the car, searched, and taken to jail in a police car.

There he was thrown in a large cell with two other volunteers and a large number of serious lawbreakers, derelicts, and drunks. When Abernathy and other friends came to arrange for bail, they were told that it was too late; the courthouse was closed for the day. But a crowd began to gather outside the Montgomery city jail, a crowd of Dexter Avenue Church members and other supporters. It soon grew so large that the jail authorities became nervous. Dr. King was released on bail after all.

But his arrest was a signal of worse things to come. More and more volunteers were arrested on similar charges. Others, less prominent and more vulnerable, were mistreated and often beaten on the ride to jail. More and more money was tied up in bail bonds, and sometimes it was a while before one could be arranged. People who had never been inside a jail in their lives were forced to spend the night on the dirty, torn mattresses or hard plank beds of crowded, unsanitary "tanks."

Then an even more serious threat to the transportation system developed. Alabama had legal standards for the condition of brakes, headlights, and other equipment on motor vehicles, but no law requiring regular official inspection. Now, suddenly, Montgomery policemen began stopping cars, inspecting them then and there, and finding all sorts of "violations."

The driver would be told that he could not continue in that condition. The city wrecker would be called to haul the car to a shop where the problem (if any) could be corrected, at the driver's expense. And the expense was usually very heavy, beyond the means of most of the volunteers.

It was getting harder, not easier, to keep the transportation system operating. There were more and more frequent breakdowns in service. More and more people were having to walk. But they were not riding the buses. And that was costing the bus company thousands upon thousands of dollars every day.

The First Violence

While this battle of wills was occurring on the car-pool front, a group of self-appointed "guardians of the Southern way of life" was getting ready to use the old weapon of illegal terror, the weapon that had been most successful in forcing blacks to accept segregation and discrimination at the beginning of the century.

Martin Luther King and some other leaders had received threatening phone calls and letters from the start. But by mid-January the "hate" mail at the King residence alone was averaging thirty-five letters a day. Many were signed "K.K.K." Others were anonymous. Some were obscene.

Toward the end of the month, a white friend warned Dr. King that plans were being made for an attempt on his life. Soon afterward he was awakened in the middle of the night by a phone call. An angry voice said, "Listen, nigger, we've taken all we want from you. Before next week, you'll be sorry you ever came to Montgomery."*

The following Monday night, the mass meeting was held at Dr. Abernathy's church and Dr. King was on the agenda. He left his wife, Coretta, and their new baby daughter, Yolanda, at home, but not alone. A member of Dr. King's congregation had volunteered to stay with Mrs. King whenever her husband had to be away at night. The two women were in the living room, watching television, at about 9:30 P.M., when they heard a heavy thump on the porch.

A few moments later there was an explosion.

By the time Dr. King had been notified and could get back to his home, there was a crowd in the yard. Police Commissioner Sellers was

―――――――
*Martin Luther King, Jr. *Stride Toward Freedom*, Perennial Library, Harper & Row, N.Y., 1964, p. 114.

The Rev. Martin Luther King, Jr., urges calmness from the porch of his home, which was damaged by a bomb that same evening. At right is Police Commissioner Clyde Sellers. Mayor W. A. Gayle (in uniform) stands behind Dr. King. (United Press International)

there and so were many white policemen. The mood of the black people in the crowd was so angry that it seemed inevitable that some sort of clash would break out at any moment.

As King got out of the car, he heard a Negro say to a policeman who was trying to push him back, "You got your thirty-eight and I got mine, so let's battle it out."* For the first time since the movement began, he noticed, blacks were carrying arms. Nonviolence which had

*Ibid, p. 116.

held up under many provocations was dissolving under this one — a terrorist attack on the family of the man the whole black community of Montgomery had accepted as their spokesman and leader.

His first thought was for Coretta and "Yoki," but once he had made sure they were unharmed, he returned to the ruined front porch, where the mayor and police commissioner were waiting. There were other white people in the crowd now — some friends, some reporters, and more and more armed policemen.

Dr. King began to speak and there was quiet. His voice was low and calm, and his words were about *agape*, or "disinterested Christian love."

"We cannot solve this problem through retaliatory violence," he said. "We must love our white brothers no matter what they do to us. We must make them know that we love them. We must meet hate with love. . . . Remember, if I am stopped, this movement will not stop, because God is with the movement."

There were shouts of "Amen!" from the crowd, which began quietly to disperse at Dr. King's request. It seemed to some observers that he had averted the omen of a bloody race war's opening skirmish.

Mayor Gayle of Montgomery offered a reward to the person or persons who would report the names of those responsible for the bombing. No one claimed the reward. Two nights later another bomb was thrown.

This time the target was the home of E. D. Nixon.

The dynamite missed the house and went off in the yard. From that time on, every leader of the MIA knew that his house might be the next target and that the aim of the bombers might not always be so poor.

The Boycott "Conspiracy"

In February, the focus of conflict moved from the car pools to the courts. The city attorney "discovered" an old law which prohibited boycotts. Warrants were issued for the arrest of over one hundred leaders of the MIA.

No attempt was made to surprise them. Notice was given in advance that the arrests were to take place on February 22. If the authorities had expected to spread fear in the upper ranks of the movement, the community's reaction must have shocked them profoundly. Men didn't wait to be arrested. They went down to the courthouse and demanded to be. Those whose names were not on the list asked to be arrested anyway.

Dr. King was in Nashville, Tennessee, giving a series of lectures at Fisk University. As soon as Dr. Abernathy called him with the news, he cancelled his lectures and flew back to Atlanta, where Coretta and the baby were staying with the senior Martin Luther Kings. He drove back to Montgomery on February 23. Again, national networks sent teams to record the spectacle of this dignified man of God, surrounded by an "honor guard" of his colleagues, arriving at the jail to claim the privilege of being booked, fingerprinted, and released on bond for the second time in his life.

The trial of the boycott conspiracy defendants began on March 19. Reporters were present from all over the United States, Europe, and even India. Religious and political leaders came from near and far. Hundreds of Montgomery's black citizens stood in the halls of the courthouse, and on the steps and sidewalks outside. Without intending it, the authorities had provided the perfect forum for an airing of the grievances that had led to the boycott in the first place.

Mrs. Rosa Parks is fingerprinted by a deputy sheriff in Montgomery on February 22, 1956. (Wide World Photos)

Defense attorneys called twenty-eight witnesses, not to testify as to whether or not the MIA was a conspiracy in violation of the law, but to show why the protest had been necessary. Many of these witnesses were poor, uneducated women, who had never stood up to speak in public. But each had a story to tell. One had been called "an ugly black ape" by a bus driver. Another had seen a black man threatened with a pistol because he didn't have the right change. Another told how her blind husband had been caught in a closing door and dragged. Another, how her husband had asked for his dime back when he was

[39]

A group of men who were arrested in February because of alleged boycott violations in Montgomery. At left stands the Rev. Ralph Abernathy. (United Press International)

ordered to the crowded rear section, and how in the argument that followed, he was shot to death.

The verdict of "guilty" was handed down by Judge Eugene Carter on March 22. As chief defendant, Martin Luther King, Jr., was fined five hundred dollars and court costs, or sentenced to 386 days at hard labor. His attorneys announced that they would appeal, and the cases of the others were continued.*

*That is, the other cases were made to depend on the outcome of Dr. King's appeal. If it was denied, they would have to stand trial. If it succeeded in reversing the verdict, they too would go free.

As the Kings left the courthouse, they were greeted by a wildly enthusiastic crowd. News cameras caught the scene as the young minister waved and his supporters burst into a chant: "We ain't gonna ride the buses no more!"

To Raise the Federal Question

By April, it seemed that there was a stalemate. The bus company was "hurting" badly. Its parent company, the National City Lines of Chicago, was eager to reach any kind of compromise that would restore its income. But the Montgomery City Lines still needed the goodwill of the City Commission in the matter of their franchise renewal, and the city authorities did not feel themselves under any pressure of time.

If anything, time was on their side. For the boycott could only continue as long as the working people of Montgomery could get back and forth to their jobs. With every passing day that was becoming more difficult. Cars were wearing out. Repair bills were growing. Drivers were giving up. And the terrible heat of an Alabama summer was still to be suffered.

The hopes of the MIA rested on the fate of Mrs. Parks's challenge of the segregation law itself. But nothing moves so slowly as that type of legal appeal. And there was no way to hurry the process. Also, there was a growing fear among attorneys involved in the movement that the state court might not rule on the "federal question" if and when it ever did rule. It might reverse the lower court on some small technical point and the case would go back for a new trial. The whole procedure would have to be repeated. Years could be spent in this way.

There was, however, one way of getting more directly to the U.S. Supreme Court. That was to bring an action in the local district (i.e., federal) court. A group of citizens might petition for an injunction against segregated seating on the grounds that it was a violation of the United States Constitution. Such an action would be heard before a three-judge panel, instead of the district judge alone.

This was required because of the seriousness of an apparent con-

The Rev. Martin Luther King, Jr., shakes hands with one of his lawyers after having been found guilty of conspiring to boycott segregated city buses in Montgomery. Dr. King's wife is standing behind him. (International News Photos)

flict between a state and a federal law. It had the advantage of saving a whole step in the appeals procedure. For one of the three judges on the panel had to be a member of the circuit, or appeals, court. An appeal from the verdict of the three-judge panel, therefore, was made directly to the U.S. Supreme Court in Washington.

Early in May, Fred Gray began to work on such a petition. He had the help and advice of some older lawyers and the promise of support from the NAACP. But even so, it was a daring and difficult step for a young man only a year out of law school. Fred Gray had taken a tremendous amount of pressure from the events of the past six months, but he was developing under that pressure with a speed that impressed everyone, including the opposition. There was some danger that he might become the sort of target Dr. King and Dr. Abernathy and E. D. Nixon had become.

One friend warned Gray to be careful in the arrangements he made with the clients who were "parties" to the petition for a three-judge panel. There was an Alabama law that penalized attorneys who came into court on behalf of clients, without those clients' permission. The offense was known as barratry, and a few years before, a black lawyer had been convicted of it and disbarred. In his case there had been a similar challenge of one of the segregation laws. Pressure had been brought to bear on some of his clients, and one had finally broken down and sworn that he had not given permission for his name to be used.

It would be wise, this friend said, for Gray to have written contracts with all parties to his action, and to be sure that all signatures were witnessed by someone other than himself. Fred Gray went one step further. At a meeting of the plaintiffs, he turned on his tape recorder and caught the voices of each of his new clients, all enthusiastic and eager for the suit.

These precautions proved very wise indeed. Hardly had the petition been filed, when efforts were made to remove the young lawyer from the scene.

He was notified by the local draft board that his ministerial exemption had been revoked and that he was eligible for immediate induction into the army. Gray was an ordained minister,* but clearly

---

*While he was earning his law degree at Western Reserve in Ohio, Gray had supported himself as pastor of a Negro church in that area.

his major occupation was that of one-man, full-time legal staff of the MIA. He appealed the ruling of the local board, and it was eventually overturned by the national draft director, General Hershey.

Meanwhile, the barratry law had been invoked against Gray. One of Gray's clients was the cook in the home of a relative of Mayor Gayle's. Someone persuaded her to swear that she had not authorized Gray to put her name on his petition. Gray was quickly indicted, and his case was called for trial in the local state court.

In this emergency, the NAACP legal staff — both national and state — was involved as defense counsel. The courtroom was crowded with spectators, some of whom had come to show support for Gray, and some who were curious about the distinguished black attorneys from Birmingham and New York. But before they had a chance to be heard, the prosecutor asked the judge to dismiss the case!

He had discovered on more careful study, he said, that the offense (sic) had been committed on federal property since the suit Gray had filed was a federal suit. State courts had no jurisdiction in such a case. The prosecutor promised that he would turn over his material to the U.S. District Attorney's office for "appropriate action."

But the U.S. District Attorney's office never found any action appropriate.

The hearing on Gray's petition was on May 11, 1956. The judges were Richard T. Rives, of the Fifth Circuit (a native son of Montgomery), Frank Johnson, the new district judge in the area (a northern Alabamian), and Seybourne Lynn, of Birmingham. Some of the same NAACP lawyers who had represented Gray were present to assist him in the argument before the panel. Their attack was on the unfairness and the inconsistency of the segregation laws, both city and state. The reply of the city attorneys was that any change in these laws would lead to violence and bloodshed.

The judges deliberated for three weeks. On June 4, their ruling was handed down. By a two-to-one vote, Judge Lynn dissenting, the segregation law as applied to public buses was found to be unconstitutional. Attorneys for the city announced that they would appeal to the U.S. Supreme Court.

The federal question had been raised in the highest tribunal of all.

The Darkest Hour

While this appeal was pending, the struggle went on in Montgomery, sometimes under a surface calm, sometimes with open violence.

There were more bombings, but they were rather amateurish affairs: a few sticks of dynamite thrown from a passing car, landing in yards where the explosion caused little serious damage. Threatening phone calls and letters still came to the leaders of the MIA. The only new tactic of the opposition was harassment of the car pools through the avenue of insurance.

Although there had been no serious accidents and no losses to the insuring companies, over and over again a policy would be cancelled without reason given. When the fourth company to cancel in four months notified the MIA that as of September 15, its vehicles would no longer be covered by liability insurance, it seemed that the end of the road had been reached. Without such insurance it was too risky to continue the car-pool system, for there were men in Alabama who were not above provoking accidents in which huge damages could be asked.

In this crisis, as so often before, help came from an unexpected, outside source. Someone called long distance to suggest that the MIA contact the world-famous insurance firm, Lloyds of London. It was done. Before September 15, new policies had been written covering the MIA "fleet."

Then the city moved directly and openly against the car pools. On October 30, Mayor Gayle instructed the city's legal department "to file such proceedings as it may deem proper to stop the operation of car pool or transportation systems growing out of the bus boycott."

Again Gray filed a petition for an injunction in the district court.

This time the petition was denied. The city lawyers' petition was granted. Subpoenas were issued for a number of MIA leaders, and a hearing was set for Tuesday, November 13.

At the mass meeting the night before the hearing, Martin Luther King explained just how serious this new threat was. He admitted that he saw little chance that the car pools could survive, and that he didn't know how the boycott could survive without the car pools.

"This may well be the darkest hour just before dawn," he told his silent, solemn audience. "We have moved all of these months with the daring faith that God was with us in our struggle. . . . We must believe that a way will be made out of no way. . . ."

The city attorneys argued next morning that the car pools were a "public nuisance" and "a private enterprise operating without a franchise." The defense denied both charges, claiming that they were a voluntary share-a-ride plan, provided as a nonprofit public service by local churches. The city was also asking damages on the grounds that more than $15,000 in revenue had been lost.*

Just before the end of the morning session, Dr. King noticed that the city attorneys, the police commissioner, and the mayor had all been called out of the room. There was an excited buzzing at the press table. A minute later, the AP reporter came to him with a slip of paper in his hand. "Here's the decision you've been waiting for," he said.

It read:

> The United States Supreme Court today affirmed a decision of a special three-judge U.S. District Court in declaring Alabama's state and local laws requiring segregation on buses un-

---

*That was an estimate of the city's 2 percent tax on bus fares, which would put the company's loss at $750,000.

[48]

constitutional. The Supreme Court acted without listening to any argument; it simply said, "the motion to affirm is granted and the Judgment is affirmed."

That night the Montgomery radio carried an announcement by the Ku Klux Klan that its members planned to demonstrate in the Negro community. There were even uglier threats spread by rumor. A letter was dropped at the King home, warning that "if you allow the niggers to go back on the buses and sit in the front seats, we're going to burn down fifty houses in one night, including yours."*

The Klan did ride. About forty carloads of white-robed and hooded Klansmen drove through Negro neighborhoods, expecting, no doubt, to see darkened houses. In the past, as Dr. King wrote in his book, "fearing death, they [the blacks] played dead." But this time it was different. Porch lights were on. Doors stood open, although it was winter. Families watched the Klan go by as if it were a parade. A few children clapped and waved.

*Martin Luther King, op cit, p. 142.

"Be Ready When the Great Day Comes"

It took from November 13 until December 20 for the mandate — the formal, written order — of the U.S. Supreme Court to reach Montgomery. During that time the boycott was officially cancelled, but no one rode the buses anyway. All sorts of temporary arrangements were made to substitute for the outlawed car pools. And the time was used to prepare the black community for the day when integrated seating would go into effect.

MIA leaders addressed meetings all over the city, in churches, clubs, and schools. They warned against any sort of provocative behavior, any gloating or boasting over the victory. Classes in role playing were held, in which a dozen or so people took the parts of drivers, or white and black passengers. Some behaved in hostile ways. Others played the role of nonviolent resisters. If the hostile roles provoked angry reactions, both kinds of behavior were discussed by the group.

Mimeographed sheets of Integrated Bus Suggestions, prepared by a white minister of the Fellowship of Reconciliation, were distributed at all classes and meetings. Here are some:*

> Not all white people are opposed to integrated buses. Accept goodwill on the part of many.
>
> The *whole* bus is now for the use of *all* people. Take a vacant seat.
>
> Demonstrate the calm dignity of our Montgomery people in your actions.

*Ibid, p. 144, et seq.

With the Supreme Court's order banning bus segregation in effect, Montgomery's black citizens decide to end their long boycott and to start riding city buses the next day. Photo shows part of the crowd in a mass meeting applauding Dr. King's recommendation that they return to the buses without violence. (Wide World Photos)

Be quiet, but friendly; proud, but not arrogant; joyous, but not boisterous.

Now for some specific suggestions:

Do not deliberately sit by a white person, unless there is no other seat.

If cursed, do not curse back. If pushed, do not push back. If struck, do not strike back, but evidence love and goodwill at all times.

For the first few days, try to get on the bus with a friend in whose nonviolence you have confidence. You can uphold one another by a glance or a prayer.

If another person is being molested, do not arise to go to his defense, but pray for the oppressor and use moral and spiritual force to carry on the struggle for justice.

If you feel you cannot take it, walk for another week or two.

There was not, unfortunately, any such preparation on the white side of the racially divided city. Indeed, the authorities seemed determined to oppose the change. Two days before the mandate came down, the City Commission issued the following statement.*

This decision in the bus case has had a tremendous impact on the customs of our people here in Montgomery. It is not an easy thing to live under a law recognized as constitutional for these many years and then have it suddenly overturned on the basis of psychology. . . . The City Commission, and we know our people are with us in this determination, will not yield one inch, but will do all in its power to oppose the integration of the Negro race with the white race in Montgomery, and will forever stand like a rock against social equality, intermarriage, and mixing of the races under God's creation and plan.

*Ibid, pp. 146-47.

Dr. Martin Luther King, Jr., is shown here riding up front on a Montgomery public bus after the Supreme Court's decision that bus segregation in Alabama is unconstitutional. Seated beside him is the Rev. Glenn Smiley of Texas. (United Press International)

On December 20, the MIA notified the bus company that service on all lines should be restored to accommodate passengers who would be riding on the following day.

At a little before 6:00 A.M., December 21, 1956, Rev. Ralph Abernathy, E. D. Nixon, and Rev. Glenn Smiley (the white minister who had prepared the suggestion sheet), all met with Dr. King at his residence. Television and newspapermen were waiting outside as the four came out and started for the bus stop.

At exactly six o'clock, the first bus turned the corner and came to a halt. The door opened. Martin Luther King stepped on and dropped his dime in the box.

"I believe you're Reverend King, aren't you?" the driver asked with a pleasant smile. "We're glad to have you this morning."

Dr. King smiled back and took a seat in the front section. Smiley sat down next to him. Abernathy and Nixon took seats nearby. Cameramen scrambled for other vacant seats from which they could record the historic scene: a white and a black minister, sitting together and chatting on a Montgomery city bus.

Backlash

That first day everything went well. There were a few unpleasant incidents, but there were also whites who went out of their way to be cordial. The *Montgomery Advertiser* reported that:

The calm but cautious acceptance of this significant change in Montgomery's way of life came without any major disturbance.

But a few days later the major disturbance came. First there was sniper fire in poorly lighted sections of the city. Then a young Negro girl was beaten by white men as she got off a bus. Then a pregnant Negro woman was shot in the leg. The City Commission suspended all runs beginning after 5:00 P.M., which meant that working people could not ride the buses home.

Inflammatory leaflets began to circulate. The Klan marched again in full regalia and burned crosses in various places. Finally, on the night of January 9, the bombers struck again.

They began with Dr. Abernathy's home. He was in Atlanta with Dr. King, preparing for the gathering out of which the Southern Christian Leadership Council was formed. A short time later, a second blast went off at his church. At intervals of about ten minutes, blast after blast was heard. Some who were waked took it for a series of sonic booms cause by some special exercise of the planes at nearby Maxwell Air Force Base.

Three Baptist churches besides Abernathy's were bombed that night, two of them almost destroyed. The home of Rev. Robert Graetz

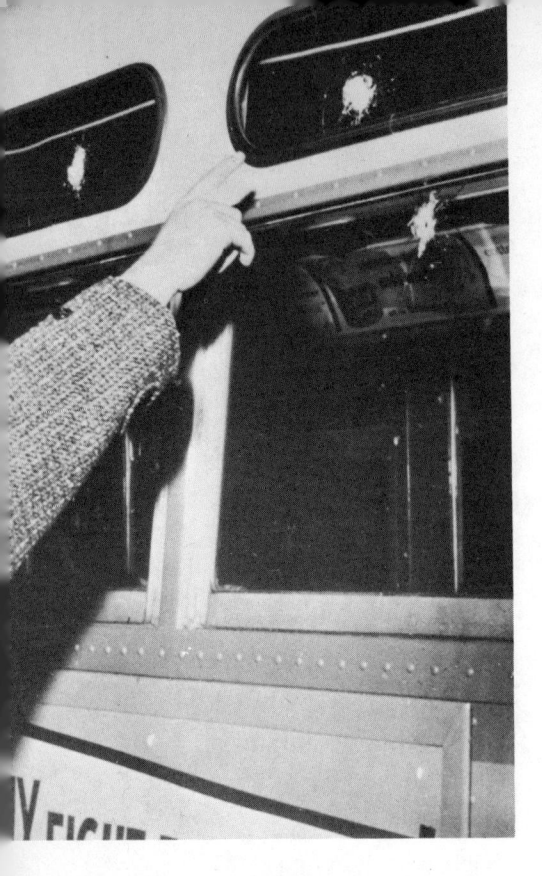

A spectator points to rifle bullet holes in a Montgomery city bus fired by an unidentified gunman. Another bus was struck by shotgun pellets, but no one was injured in either incident. (Wide World Photos)

was bombed for the second time and almost destroyed.* No one was killed or severely injured, but the limits of nonviolent patience had been reached by many.

E. D. Nixon stood on his front porch with a Winchester rifle in his arms. A car drove slowly down the block and swerved to flash its lights on him. His finger was on the trigger, when the car swerved the other way, speeded up, turned at the next corner, and disappeared.

On January 10, the decent white community of Montgomery found its voice at last. Ministers, editors, and businessmen made public

---

*Graetz, a white Lutheran minister, was the only white man invited to serve on the executive board of the MIA.

[56]

statements condemning the bombings. But in spite of this strong, if somewhat tardy opposition, the apostles of terror continued their tactics. On January 28, a Negro-owned filling station close to Dr. King's house was bombed, as was the residence of an elderly hospital worker in the neighborhood. An unexploded bundle of twelve sticks of dynamite was found smoldering under the porch of the King residence.

The owner of the filling station had reported the license number of a car full of white men who had stopped on the night of January 9 and asked directions to Abernathy's home or church. Acting on this lead, the FBI had traced the car and eventually arrested seven men. They were charged with the bombings of January 9, and some — if not all — signed confessions.

The Final Act

The trial of these men was the final act in the long drama of Montgomery's boycott movement. They were defended by John Blue Hill, a member of the leading political family in the region. His fee was said to be $5,000 per defendant, paid in cash before he would move in the case. (There was a joke going the rounds that it was John Blue Hill who stopped the bombings, not the FBI, because Hill simply made it too expensive.) The sum of money — $35,000 — was collected by men and women, and even children, who rattled plastic buckets with slogans like "Save Our Southern Way of Life" on downtown street corners for weeks before the trial.

Hill's defense consisted almost entirely of an attack on the leaders of the MIA. Not one of the accused men was ever called to the stand. Instead, he subpoenaed Dr. King, Dr. Abernathy, E. D. Nixon, and others. Hill's questions to Dr. King were constantly directed toward the story that King had once asked a white woman to marry him. The judge ruled such questioning irrelevant and instructed the jury to disregard it, but the oldest and most irrational of prejudices had been stirred. Despite the signed confessions and the best efforts of the prosecutor, the jury returned a verdict of "not guilty" and the defenders left the courtroom like triumphant champions of the "Southern way of life."

Aftermath

Integration of Montgomery buses proceeded without further trouble, after the bombers' trial. Drivers were carefully schooled in courtesy to black passengers, and all signs referring to segregated seating were removed.

The cases against the other five indicted bombers were dropped in a general amnesty which also pardoned all the boycott-conspiracy defendants except Dr. King, who paid his five-hundred-dollar fine.

There were some gains in the integration of other aspects of life. A few labor unions integrated their membership, and a number of black unionists were elected to the joint AFL-CIO Executive Board for Southern Alabama. There was more courtesy extended to Negro customers in Montgomery stores. Newspapers began to use the titles "Mr." and "Mrs." when referring to blacks, a practice which was frowned on in 1956.

On the other hand, the City Commission passed new ordinances which forbade black and white children playing games together or using the same public parks. School integration did not proceed with "deliberate" or any other kind of speed.

The most important consequences of the Montgomery movement were felt in other places in the years after 1956.

Nonviolent protest became the philosophy of the sit-ins and the freedom rides by which young black and white people changed so many patterns of southern living during the late 1950's and early 1960's.

The Southern Christian Leadership Council headed campaigns for voter registration in the South, and eventually attacked the problems of housing and job discrimination in such northern centers as Chicago

A photograph taken in 1965 shows Dr. King and Mrs. Rosa Parks reminiscing over the Montgomery Bus Boycott. (United Press International)

and Detroit. In 1967, the SCLC undertook to organize poor people of all races — black, brown, red, and white — to petition the government in Washington for the kind of justice that would make democracy meaningful in their lives. In the last stages of preparation for a great "Poor People's March," Martin Luther King, Jr., was killed by an assassin's bullet before his fortieth birthday.

    The movement he helped to found continues under the leadership of Rev. Ralph Abernathy and Coretta Scott King. And the flag of the Confederacy, not that of the United States, still flies over the dome of the state capitol which looks down Dexter Avenue to the church where the Montgomery boycott movement was born.

Index

Abernathy, Rev. Ralph, 13, 35, 38, 44, 61
  and bombings, 55, 57-58
  and end of boycott, 54
  at Holt Street Church meeting, 26
  and King's arrest, 33
  and MIA founding, 20-21
Advertiser (Montgomery), 17-18, 32, 55
AFL-CIO Executive Board of Southern Alabama, black unionists on, 59
Agape, 37
Alabama State College, 9*n*., 14
Azbell, Joe, 17-18

Baptist Ministerial Alliance, 13
Barratry offense, 44-45
Baton Rouge car pool plan, 27-29
Bennett, Rev. L. Roy, 14, 16
Black community of Montgomery, differences in, 9
Black militants, and "Uncle Toms," 9
Bombers' trial, 58-59
Bombings, 47, 55-56
  of Abernathy home, 55
  arrest and trial of leaders of, 57-58
  of Graetz home, 55-56
  integration following, 59
  of King home, 35-37
  of Nixon home, 37
  white community's reaction to, 56-57
Boston University, 21
Boycott, Montgomery bus:
  arrest and trial of leaders of, 38-41
  backlash following, 55-57
  cancelling of, 50, 54
  continuation of, 23
  financial support for, 31
  Holt Street Church meeting and, 24-26
  integration following, 59
  planning of, 12-17
  publicity for, 17-18, 25, 31
  success of, 19-20

(*See also*: Montgomery Improvement Association; Car pools)
Boycott-conspiracy defendants:
  pardoning of, 59
  trial of, 38-41
Brotherhood of Sleeping Car Porters, 8
Brown v. Board of Education of Topeka (1954), 5
Bus boycott (*see* Boycott, Montgomery bus)
Bus company (*see* Montgomery City Lines)

Car pools:
  harassment of, 33-34, 47
  organization and operation of, 27-30
  outlawing of, 47-48, 50
  problems of, 29-30, 42
Carter, Judge Eugene, 40
Chicago, SCLC activities in, 59
Circuit (appeals) court, 43
City Commission (Montgomery), 32, 42
  and MIA demands, 27
  post-boycott actions of, 55, 59
  statement on bus desegregation decision, 52
Colvin, Claudette, 2, 9
Confederate flag on Alabama capitol, 61
Council on Human Relations (Montgomery), 9, 11
"Cradle of the Confederacy," 3
Crenshaw, Jack, 2
Crozer Theological Seminary, 21

Detroit, SCLC activities in, 59-61
Dexter Avenue Baptist Church, 13, 15, 33, 61
Durr, Clifford, 11-12, 19

Federal Bureau of Investigation (FBI), and bombings, 57-58

Federal district court, 42-43
"Federal question" in bus segregation law challenge, 42
Fellowship of Reconciliation, 50
First Baptist Church, 13
Fisk University, 38
Freedom rides, 59
French, Rev. E. N., 20-22

Gayle, Mayor, 37, 45, 47-48
Gone with the Wind (film), 19
"Goon squads," myth of, 18-19, 31
Graetz, Rev. Robert, 55-56
Gray, Fred, 11, 12
   and car pool outlawing, 47-48
   and defense of Mrs. Parks, 19-20
   and petition to federal district court, 43-46
   trial of, 45-46

Hershey, General, 45
Hill, John Blue, 58
Holt Street Baptist Church, 17, 24-26
Housing discrimination, SCLC and, 59
Hubbard, Rev. H. H., 13

Insurance companies and car pool harassment, 47
Integrated Bus Suggestions, 50-52
Integration:
   gains in following boycott, 59
   slowness of in schools, 5-7
Interdenominational Ministerial Alliance, 14, 16

Jim Crow laws, 3-5, 7
   Gray's challenge to, 20, 42, 45-46
   Supreme Court rulings against, 5, 48-50, 52
Job discrimination, SCLC and, 59
Johnson, Judge Frank, 45

King, Coretta Scott, 35, 37, 38, 61
King, Dr. Martin Luther Jr., 13, 15, 16, 19, 44, 57
   assassination of, 61
   and bombers' trial, 58
   bombing of home of, 35-37
   and boycott conspiracy, 38-41, 59
   and car pools, 27-28, 33, 47
   educational background of, 21
   and end of boycott, 54
   at Holt Street Baptist Church meeting 24, 25-26
   and Montgomery Improvement Association, 21-23
   and SCLC founding, 55
   and *Stride Toward Freedom*, 23n., 35, 49, 50-52
   threats against, 35, 49
   white religious leaders and, 32
King, Mr. and Mrs. Martin Luther Sr., 38
King, Yolanda ("Yoki"), 35, 37, 38
Ku Klux Klan (KKK), 35, 49, 55

Labor unions, integration in, 59
Lewis, Rufus, 28, 29
Lloyds of London, 47
Lynn, Judge Seybourne, 45

Mason and Dixon's Line, 5
Miss White's school for Negro girls, 10
Montgomery Advertiser, 17-18, 32, 55
Montgomery boycotts:
   of 1900-1902, 7
   of 1955-1956 (*see* Boycott, Montgomery bus)
Montgomery branch of NAACP, 1-2, 8, 23
Montgomery City Commission (*see* City Commission)
Montgomery City Lines, 42
   drivers' discrimination on, 1-2
   economic losses of, 34, 48n.
   and MIA demands, 27
Montgomery Council on Human Relations, 9, 11
Montgomery Improvement Association (MIA):

[63]

arrest and trial of leaders, 38-41
and boycott, attempts to stop, 32-33, 47
demands of, 23, 27
financial support for, 31
founding of, 20-23
Rev. Graetz on board of, 56n.
Hill's attack on, 58
and segregation law challenge, 42, 45
and Supreme Court decision, activities following, 50-54
threats against leaders of, 47
transportation committee of, 28-29
(See also: Boycott, Montgomery bus; Car pools)
Morehouse College, 21

National Association for the Advancement of Colored People (NAACP), 7, 12
Alabama state branch of, 7-8
and boycott, support for, 31
and Gray's petition, 44, 45
Montgomery branch of, 1-2, 8, 23
National City Lines of Chicago, 42
Nixon, E. D., 2, 3, 17-18, 44
and boycott, end of, 54, 56
and boycott, planning for, 7-9, 11, 13-15
and bombers' trial, 58
at Holt Street Church meeting, 24-25
and MIA, founding of, 20-22
Nonviolent protest, 59

Parks, Mrs. Rosa, 9-10, 17
arrest of, 1-3
and Gray's defense, 19-20, 42
and Martin Luther King, 15, 25
and MIA, 22, 24
and E. D. Nixon, 11-12
Police protection in boycott, 18-19

"Poor People's March," 61

Rives, Judge Richard T., 45
Robinson, Mrs. Jo Ann, 14, 16

Segregation laws, unconstitutionality of, 5, 48-50, 52. See also Jim Crow laws
Sellers, Police Commissioner, 19, 25, 35, 37, 48
Sit-ins, 59
Smiley, Rev. Glenn, 54
Integrated Bus Suggestions of, 50-52
Sniper fire following boycott, 55
Southern Christian Leadership Conference (SCLC), 55, 59-61
Streetcars, boycott of (1900-1902), 7
Stride Toward Freedom, 23n., 35, 49, 50-52. See also King, Dr. Martin Luther Jr.
Supreme Court (U.S.), 12, 42-43, 46
desegregation decisions of, 5, 48-50, 52

Taxicab companies, Negro-owned, 17, 27, 28
Transportation committee of MIA, 28-29. See also Car pools

"Uncle Toms," black militants' views of, 9
Unions (labor), integration in, 59

Voter registration in South, SCLC and, 59

West, Mrs. A. W., 28
Western Reserve University, 44n.
White community of Montgomery, reaction to bombings, 56-57
Wilson, Rev. A. W., 24
Women's Political Council, 14